The ethereum merge had happened:

And marks a new era for greener cryptos and blockchain

By Richard Tucker

Table of content

introduction

The Ethereum blockchain is getting a significant upgrade, known as "the Merge," and the cryptocurrency community is buzzing about what may turn out to be a watershed moment for the nascent digital currency industry. The Merge, which went live on Thursday, is expected to significantly lessen the environmental effect of cryptocurrency mining and increase its usefulness more generally as a means of conducting financial transactions, among other applications, according to cryptocurrency aficionados.
But what precisely is the merge, and how can it affect the development of cryptocurrency?

After the Ethereum "Merge," a new era for blockchain technology and greener cryptocurrencies began.

The Ethereum "Merge" has taken place, ushering in a new age for more environmentally friendly cryptocurrencies and blockchains. Ethereum has switched to a PoS mechanism that uses less energy.
-Copies of works
According to its platform, Ethereum, the second-largest cryptocurrency in the world, has undergone a substantial transition that will improve its technology to reduce carbon emissions by more than 99.9%.

The "Merge" transfer has been completed, Ethereum creator Vitalik Buterin said on Thursday.
"We concluded, then!
... Best wishes to everyone who is merging.For the Ethereum ecosystem, this is a significant occasion. In a tweet, he stated
It indicates that its blockchain technology has advanced from the highly energy-intensive one utilized by its competitor.

While the price of Ethereum's token, Ether (ETH), has increased in the past two months due to the shift, not everyone is in favor of it.

chapter 1: What is the merge

The Merge was the union of Ethereum's new proof-of-stake consensus layer, the Beacon Chain, with its original execution layer, the Mainnet, which has been around since the platform's inception. It made it unnecessary to use energy-intensive mining and allowed the network to be protected using staked ETH instead. More scalability, security, and sustainability made it a very exciting step in bringing the Ethereum goal to life.

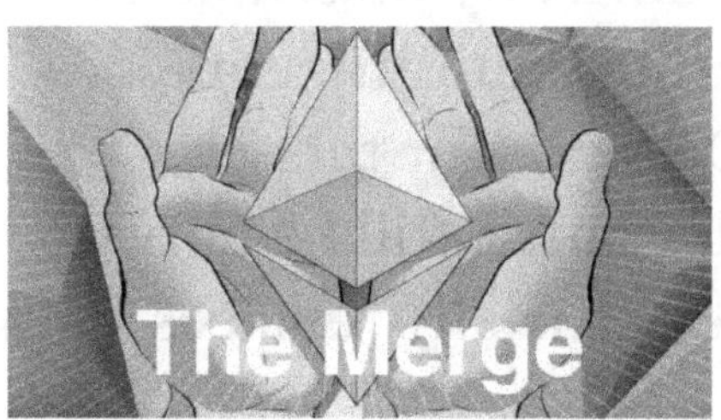

The long-awaited "Merge upgrade" is Ethereum's transition to a "Proof-of-Stake" consensus mechanism from its existing "Proof-of-Work" system. The Bellatrix and Paris upgrades are the two steps that lead to The Merge. The Merge got its formal start on September 6, 2022, at 11:34:47 UTC. A consensus layer network improvement is Bellatrix. Paris, the execution layer that will change Ethereum from proof-of-work to proof-of-stake, will come after Bellatrix. A certain event will occur in Paris.Given how severely the proof-of-work hash rate depends on the Total Difficulty threshold, also known as the Terminal Total Difficulty (TTD), the precise date of Paris is still unknown. The total difficulty threshold for the last block to be mined in Ethereum is known as TTD. TTD stands for the set number of hashes that must still be mined before Proof-of-Stake officially replaces them.

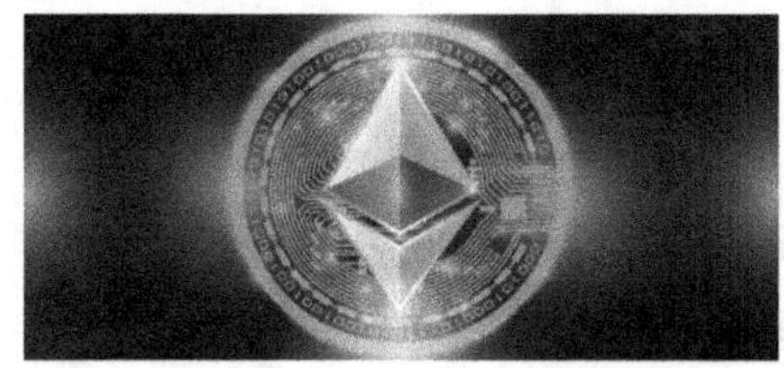

The Beacon Chain was first delivered apart from Mainnet. While the Beacon Chain functioned in parallel using proof-of-stake, the Ethereum Mainnet, with all of its accounts, balances, smart contracts, and blockchain information, continued to be protected by proof-of-work. When these two systems ultimately converged during The Merge, proof-of-stake completely superseded proof-of-work.

Imagine The spacecraft Ethereum was launched before it was fully prepared for an interstellar journey. The neighborhood constructed a new engine and a fortified hull using the Beacon Chain. It was time to change out the old engine with the new one mid flight after extensive testing. This allowed the current spacecraft to incorporate the new, more effective engine, allowing it to travel some major light years and take on the cosmos.

From its inception until The Merge, the Ethereum Mainnet was protected by proof-of-work. This made it possible for the Ethereum blockchain that we are all accustomed to—complete with transactions, smart contracts, accounts, etc.—to be created in July 2015.

Throughout the development of Ethereum, programmers planned for the eventual switch from proof-of-work to proof-of-stake. The Beacon Chain was established as a second blockchain that operates concurrently with the mainnet on December 1, 2020.

Transactions on the mainnet were not initially processed by the Beacon Chain.

Instead, it was deciding on active validators and their account balances in order to obtain agreement on its own state. It was time for the Beacon Chain to agree on actual data after lengthy testing. The Beacon Chain took over as the consensus engine for the whole network's data after The Merge, including execution layer transactions and account balances.

The Beacon Chain was formally used as the basis for block production after the Merge. Blocks can no longer be created validly by mining. Instead, the proof-of-stake validators have taken on this function and are now in charge of processing all transactions for validity and submitting blocks.

The Merge did not erase any history. The complete transactional history of Ethereum was integrated when the mainnet and the beacon chain converged.
After the Ethereum network successfully completed its transition to the proof-of-stake consensus mechanism, popularly known as the "merge," the price of ether dropped on Thursday.
According to Coin Metrics, the price of ether dropped as low as $1,459.00 before dropping by 5.6% to $1,501.88. Traders had anticipated that the price would drop after the transition late Wednesday night.

It is crucial to understand that the merger has already been priced in significant part, according to Anto Paroian, CEO of cryptocurrency hedge fund ARK36. "Since its June lows, Ethereum has already increased by more than 100%. Therefore, it appears likely that the upswing may not be sustained if the merger proves to have an impact on Ethereum's price behavior.

Ether surged to start the second half of the year after falling in value along with other risk assets during the first half, and has subsequently outperformed bitcoin. Compared to bitcoin's 27% growth, it gained about 70% just in July, according to Coin Metrics. Compared to bitcoin's loss of about 17%, it dropped by roughly 9.3% in August.

According to Paroian, "many investors anticipate it to be a'sell the news' type of event, meaning that, after the initial surge, we may actually see the price of Ethereum decline within the next few days or weeks. This is especially true given that, like the rest of the cryptocurrency markets, ETH is still heavily influenced by the unfavorable macroeconomic outlook.

Investors have been praising Ethereum's anticipated technological upgrade for months because it would allow ether to become a yield-generating asset and strengthen network security while using less energy. It has been hailed as one of the pivotal milestones in the brief history of cryptography.

A common trade that many in the cryptocurrency industry have been keeping an eye on involves investors purchasing spot ether and shorting ether perpetual futures in order to obtain free tokens of the "forked" version of Ethereum without being exposed to the ether price. According to some observers, trading should end following the merger.

Jason Lau, chief operating officer of Okcoin, told CNBC's "Crypto World" on Thursday that since the merger has taken place, investors and traders are positioning themselves to avoid it.

In contrast, asset managers and holders are putting themselves in a better position to win a longer-term game, he continued.

"The Ethereum merging is actually only one step in a lengthy sequence of improvements that will increase the network's scalability and speed."
The market is still primarily macro-driven, though. For the majority of the morning, the price of ether was largely unchanged, but it began to decline along with stocks, notably the Nasdaq Composite, which fell 1.4%. Bitcoin fell by less than 1%, reaching an all-time high correlation with equities this year.
The ethereum "merge" is making cryptocurrency bulls happy.

Let's get to it: the year has not been kind to cryptocurrencies or their devoted followers. The biggest token by far, bitcoin, has dropped around 70% from its peak almost a year ago. This is also true of ether, the second-largest coin and member of the Ethereum blockchain.

But the sophisticated Ethereum network software upgrade known as the "merge" has been the topic of much discussion among crypto enthusiasts for months.

According to the charity that created the network, the merger will, in essence, move the Ethereum network's fundamental infrastructure toward being more environmentally friendly by decreasing its carbon footprint by99%. That's the short story, however. It required years of testing and study to really get it off, and it wasn't certain what would transpire since, like so many other things in crypto-land, nothing like it had ever happened.

If the merger goes well, the ethereum network, which hosts the whole community of NFTs (non-fungible tokens), should continue to operate as usual while using far

less power and, according to proponents, becoming more secure.
Deep philosophical divisions exist among the cryptographic community over the usefulness of the underlying technology.

According to Laura Shin, presenter of the "Unchained" podcast, "Ethereum and Bitcoin have extremely different cultures." Despite the fact that, as Ethereum recently showed, it is theoretically possible for Bitcoin to change its architecture, "bitcoinists see proof-of-work as a preferable manner of safeguarding the network."

But thus far, it looks like the integration went off without a hitch.
The initial method of bitcoin mining, called proof of work, consumes a significant amount of energy. The initial method of bitcoin mining, called proof of work, consumes a significant amount of energy.

The well-known cryptocurrency network Ethereum has finished a long-awaited software update known as the Merge, switching to a more environmentally friendly foundation after years of delays, arguments, and frenzied experimentation.

The most important platform in the cryptocurrency sector is undoubtedly Ethereum, a layer of software infrastructure that serves as the foundation for thousands of apps that manage more than $50 billion in consumer cash. The change is anticipated to lower Ethereum's energy usage and pave the way for later upgrades that would make the system more user-friendly and affordable.

Engineers and academics who worked on the Merge had met to commemorate the achievement when celebrations broke out on a YouTube webcast. In a depressing year for cryptocurrency, which saw a cataclysmic market meltdown wipe out over $1 trillion from the sector and drive some well-known crypto firms into bankruptcy, it was a rare moment of happiness.

As he rejoiced with his coworkers, Danny Ryan, an Ethereum researcher who worked on the merge, stated, "This is going as well as it could so far."
Crypto users were alerted to any issues that would make the transfer more difficult.

An error with the merge may endanger the whole crypto business, destroy start-ups, and plunge the market into chaos. As a precaution, the cryptocurrency exchange Coinbase declared in August that it would halt some Ethereum deposits and withdrawals during the Merge.
In interviews conducted before the merge, Ethereum developers said that they had planned for setbacks but minimized the likelihood of a complete system failure.

“."I don't want to say that everything will go off without a hitch," said Tim Beiko, an employee of the Ethereum Foundation, a non-profit that supports platform upkeep. "Because we've done this so many times previously, we're kind of certain we won't encounter network-level concerns."
The Merge's technical specifications are quite intricate. However, the procedure ultimately comes down to a change in the way bitcoin transactions are confirmed.

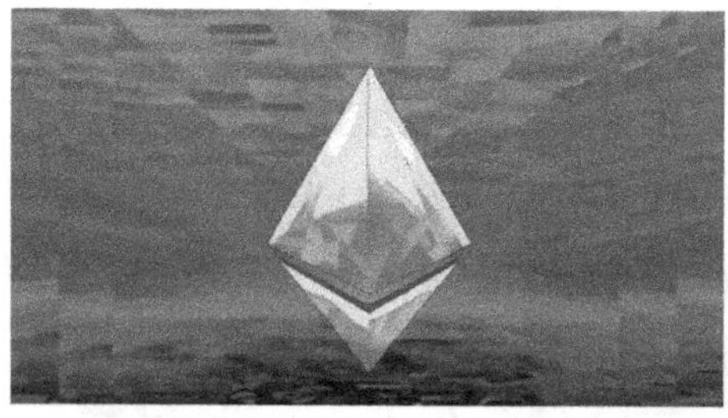

Chapter 2

When is it supposed to happen and why now?

According to blockchain specialist Merav Ozair, the Merge is taking place now because Ethereum is developed enough to manage financial transactions, hold non-fungible tokens, trade cryptocurrencies, and host smart contracts. But according to engineers, speeding up the process of adding data to the blockchain might make those and other transactions considerably faster.

According to Ozair, creator of the start-up business Blockchain Intelligence, Ethereum can do 15 transactions per second in its current state. The blockchain may potentially process up to 100,000 transactions per second, which is "far above and beyond what Visa and Mastercard can achieve," according to her, assuming the merger is successful.

The Merge's potential to cut carbon emissions in what ways? Transactions on a blockchain network aren't checked by a bank, credit card provider, or other third party. Instead, it makes use of a network of computers that compete to find solutions to challenging issues in return for tokens. The "proof of work" procedure, which is required to verify transactions on the Ethereum blockchain, requires thousands of computers.

Large quantities of electricity are needed to keep all those potent server machines running at once. The annual energy consumption of the Ethereum blockchain is around 112 terawatt hours, or nearly the same as that required to power the Netherlands. About 53 metric tons of damaging carbon emissions are released into the environment yearly as a result of this level of energy use, which is equal to what Singapore generates in a year.

The Proof-of-Stake system, which The Merge introduces, takes the place of the Proof-of-Work system. In that arrangement, cryptocurrency owners who identify themselves as "validators" offer a portion of their coins in return for the privilege of being picked at random to validate transactions and record them on a new block. We consume fewer terawatt-hours because proof of stake requires fewer users to check transactions on their computers. The Merge is anticipated to lower the energy usage of the Ethereum blockchain by 99.9% via proof-of-stake, according to its inventors.The Proof-of-Stake system, which The Merge introduces, takes the place of the

Proof-of-Work system. In that arrangement, cryptocurrency owners who identify themselves as "validators" offer a portion of their coins in return for the privilege of being picked at random to validate transactions and record them on a new block. We consume fewer terawatt-hours because proof of stake requires fewer users to check transactions on their computers.

The Merge is anticipated to lower the energy usage of the Ethereum blockchain by 99.9% via proof-of-stake, according to its inventors.The Proof-of-Stake system, which The Merge introduces, takes the place of the Proof-of-Work system. In that arrangement, cryptocurrency owners who identify themselves as "validators" offer a portion of their coins in return for the privilege of being picked at random to validate transactions and record them on a new block. We consume fewer terawatt-hours because proof of stake requires fewer users to check transactions on their computers.

The Merge is anticipated to lower the energy usage of the Ethereum blockchain by 99.9% via proof-of-stake, according to its inventors.

Will the merger make cryptocurrency use safer? Yes, most likely. Since December 2020, Ethereum developers have effectively been operating two distinct blockchains concurrently. While the mainnet version continued to operate as usual with proof of work, the beacon version was used to test the proof-of-stake mechanism. However, having both versions active provided twice as many access points for prospective Ethereum attacks.

Now that the merge is complete, the mainnet has been erased, and Beacon is the only place where financial transactions may take place. A limited pool of validators and deleting one version of the chain will lessen the likelihood that a hacker can damage the blockchain, according to the creators.

Because they haven't been thoroughly evaluated, it's crucial to remember that these improvements haven't yet demonstrated that they make accounts safer. On the website of the foundation, Ethereum developers have published a warning outlining possible hacking tactics for defrauding users of the virtual currency.

Are there any dangers or drawbacks? According to Bryan Daugherty, the worldwide public policy director for the BSV Blockchain Association, switching to a proof-of-stake system would probably result in haves and have-nots among validators and everyone else who utilizes ethereum.

This is due to the fact that in order to become an ethereum validator, a person must deposit at least 32 ether, or $52,000, and consent to keep those tokens locked away in a separate account. According to Daugherty, anyone who doesn't possess that much bitcoin is unable to operate as an ethereum transaction validator under those regulations.

The way he saw it, the idea was to stop mining altogether and give the money to the people who held the most positions.

The validators could regret agreeing to store ether in exchange, especially if the value of ether drops significantly and someone decides to sell, according to Daugherty.

On Thursday, Ethereum finally and successfully made the switch to a proof-of-stake (PoS) mechanism amid much ado and hoopla. The second-largest cryptocurrency in the world has fundamentally switched to a 99.95% less energy-intensive method. Following the integration, the price of ETH was $1,606, up by just 0.24% over the preceding 24 hours.

"During the integration, no notable price changes were seen. The price fluctuation in the upcoming months would be fascinating to watch, though, according to Amanjot Malhotra, Country Head-India, Bitay.

For everyday investors, there won't be any obvious changes after the merger. The transaction charges, or "gas fees," are still at pre-merge levels. The ETH network's transactional speed won't increase much either. Prior to the merge, mining one ETH block took around 13 seconds; after the merge, it will take 12 seconds.

However, because PoS promotes higher scalability, it has a significant influence on the development community. Ethereum now has a commanding lead in the worldwide battle for blockchain and Web 3.0 development, with more than 3,500 active decentralized apps and a $60 billion ecosystem created on this network.

However, as WazirX vice president Rajagopal Menon notes, "This merger provides the path to solve the current challenges of scalability or excessive gas prices in future upgrades. One of the major advantages of the merger is the sharply decreased ETH issuance, sometimes known as the "triple-halving" of ETH.

Menon is alluding to the significant reduction in the daily ETH issuance. The daily ETH generation ceiling will be set at 1,600 from around 13,000 ETH per day before the integration.
The ETH devotees are anticipating "the surge, the verge, the purging, and the splurge" now that the merging is complete. Menon went on.

Notably, the merging is only the first of five more enhancements that will be implemented by 2026. The surge, or the following stage, will add sharding into the Ethereum ecosystem and supercharge the Ethereum blockchain so that it can process large numbers of transactions in a matter of seconds. Sharding will dramatically increase the speed to handle one million of them per second, up from the current rate of 15-20 per second.

However, in an effort to increase their faltering trade volumes, cryptocurrency exchanges like Giottus and CoinSwitch Kuber are offering incentives to draw investors. For instance, beginning on Friday, Giottus will stop charging any fees for the ETH/INR trading pair for the next seven days. "Ethereum Trading League" by CoinSwitch Kuber, with a prize fund of Rs.

After the integration, Ethereum's miners, who oversaw block validation in its earlier

PoW incarnation, have formally said goodbye. These ETH validators, who earned nearly $19 billion last year by mining the cryptocurrency, are understandably alarmed. There have been discussions of a hard fork, or an irrevocable split of the blockchain to create a new system. It is anticipated to happen within the next few hours and has received some backing from well-known companies like Coinbase.

But because of the strong support that coalesced behind the merger, the momentum surrounding it is comparatively weak. Most experts predict that its embers will eventually extinguish.

Om Malviya, president of Tezos India, explains, "Given the difficulty of such a transformation, it will take a long time. Forking is unavoidable when it comes to the actual use case of The Merge. This event might be described as a ruse to promote Ethereum. But once the transformation occurs, its long-term effects will only become more obvious and plain.

Staking will now take on newfound significance given that the whole ETH ecosystem will now function on locked or staked ETH. However, as ETH is staked more and issued less, according to Minal Thukral, executive vice president, Growth and Strategy, CoinDCX, the impact of the lower ETH supply won't be seen for some time.

After the merging, users shouldn't anticipate having any problems getting their staked ETH out because it will be locked up for around a year. However, they may earn up to 7% a year on this frozen ETH.

Proof of Work

Members of the network fight for the opportunity to be selected to add their copy of transactions to the ledger on a blockchain that uses Proof of Work as its consensus method.

They do this by choosing a lengthy string of letters and numbers at random from among the infinite number of conceivable possibilities. The more guesses you can make per second and the faster you can find the correct answer, the more powerful your computer network becomes.

When someone provides the correct response, they are encouraged to submit their copy of the ledger for community review before it is put on the blockchain, and they are compensated with a certain amount of money.

The community would reject it as inaccurate and the person would forfeit their award if they attempted to game the system by creating a dishonest record of transactions. In practice, there is a carrot for fair play and a stick for dishonest behavior.

While someone would need to have the computational capacity to control at least 51% of the network in order to successfully game the system, this is feasible, but it would be exceedingly expensive.

Proof of Work, which is used by Bitcoin, is criticised for its impact on the environment. For example, the Bitcoin network is thought to use more energy than the entire country of Argentina.

The much-anticipated "Ethereum Merge" is now finished after several delays. The second phase of the procedure took place today, September 15.

The core operation of Ethereum, the second-largest cryptocurrency in the world after Bitcoin, has recently been modified.

What is the Ethereum merge, though, and why is it significant? Here is an explanation of what it all means and why it matters.

Keep in mind that investing in cryptocurrencies is entirely speculative, meaning your entire cash is always at risk.

Your financial losses might be partial or whole. Since there is no regulation of cryptocurrency in the UK, you probably won't be able to seek compensation if something goes wrong.

In the UK, cryptocurrencies are unregulated and quite volatile. There are no consumer safeguards. A profit tax may be imposed. Two merge into one. The change that has occurred today is significant in the cryptosphere.

It essentially comes down to how transactions are logged onto Ethereum's blockchain, which serves as an unchangeable log of all transactions.

There have been two concurrently functioning versions of Ethereum since the year 2020. One has relied on a novel approach, while the other has used the conventional way of documenting transactions.

The two versions were combined into one today, embracing the new paradigm for record-keeping. The sequence of events is detailed below.

Two key cryptocurrency ideas must be understood in order to comprehend the differences between the two versions: Cryptocurrencies and consensus procedures

The workings of a blockchain A conventional bank maintains a sizable ledger of every transaction involving its clients. The information in this ledger is crucial.

It informs the bank, for instance, which customers have how much money in each account, who has paid and received money, and so on. A centralized ledger is the name given to this list of records. Nobody may claim to have completed a transaction or to have more money than they actually have.

In comparison, a blockchain is a "decentralized ledger." This indicates that the information is held by regular individuals who volunteer to maintain it, rather than a financial entity like a bank. It keeps a complete record of every transaction and is impenetrable, giving a clear picture of who owns what assets.
So why would anyone voluntarily contribute to blockchain maintenance?

The solution is that a select few fortunate volunteers can receive huge rewards. The blockchain's "consensus mechanism"—more on that in a moment—determines who receives the rewards.

Every volunteer has a copy of the blockchain that they own independently and on their own. Each person updates this in accordance with transactions that are "broadcast" to them as users of the blockchain's network. They update their copies of the ledger when they are informed of revisions.

The ledger copies should all agree as long as no one makes any false statements regarding the contents of an account. But why would you believe that online strangers who you don't know are being truthful about their or others' account balances of virtual currency?

Once more, the blockchain's consensus process is at the center of this, so let's examine what a consensus mechanism is and why it's important.

Consensus mechanism

A blockchain's consensus process makes sure that everyone participating in maintaining records of transactions is being truthful and isn't attempting to pretend that there is more money in their or other accounts than there really is.

The way it works is that a network member is selected to have their copy of the ledger serve as the recognized record of transactions. A majority of members (51%) or more must concur that their record is accurate.

Therefore, you would need to have control over at least 51% of the networked devices in order to game the system. Depending on the consensus process used, this would need either a huge amount of computational power or a lot of money to accomplish.

Ethereum's initial consensus algorithm was based on Proof of Work. In 2016, the network was divided into two "forks," one of which continued to use Proof of Work and the other of which switched to Proof of Stake. Since the merger, Ethereum has solely used the Proof of Stake consensus algorithm.

Members of the network fight for the opportunity to be selected to add their copy of transactions to the ledger on a blockchain that uses Proof of Work as its consensus method.

They do this by choosing a lengthy string of letters and numbers at random from among the infinite number of conceivable possibilities. Your ability to make more guesses per second and the speed at which you arrive at the correct answer will increase with the strength of your computer network.

When someone provides the correct response, they are encouraged to submit their copy of the ledger for community review before it is put on the blockchain, and they are compensated with a certain amount of money.

The community would reject it as inaccurate and the person would forfeit their award if they attempted to game the system by creating a dishonest record of transactions. In practice, there is a carrot for fair play and a stick for dishonest behavior.

While someone would need to have the computational capacity to control at least 51% of the network in order to successfully game the system, this is feasible, but it would be exceedingly expensive.
Bitcoin's Proof of Work algorithm is criticized for its environmental effects. For

instance, it is estimated that the Bitcoin network consumes more energy than Argentina as a whole.

Proof of Stake

Proof of Stake requires participants to use their own cryptocurrency holdings as security in exchange for the opportunity to have their transaction history made public and get incentives.

Since no energy-intensive processing needs to be done, it is thought to be more environmentally friendly. It is also seen to be more equitable because awards aren't limited to those who can afford large computing arrays.

Your odds of becoming the next person to upload their copy of the ledger to the blockchain increase with the amount you wager.

As with Proof of Work, anyone who tries to game the system should be exposed by the community for doing so and forfeit the assets they gambled for the chance they'd created for themselves.

Although it benefits the environment, it does so at the expense of those who can afford to stake the most cryptocurrency, giving more wealth to the already wealthy.

Chapter 3

What Does Ethereum's Transition to Proof of Stake Mean for Polygon?

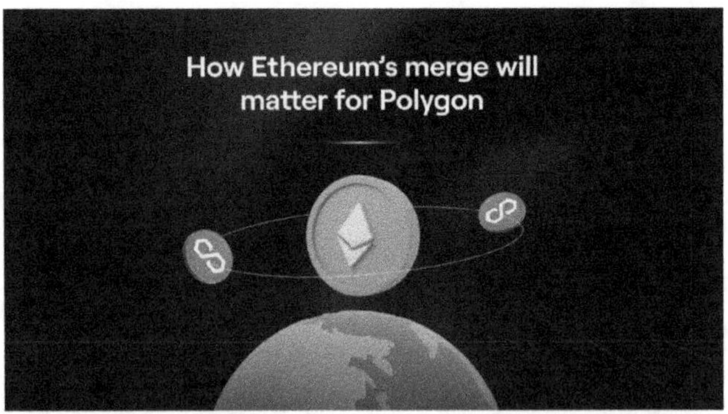

We felt it would be good to stop for a moment and appreciate how far Web3 has come in light of Ethereum's impending transition to proof of stake (PoS), which is scheduled to occur in the middle of September. It's time to honor the designers and visionaries who have toiled tirelessly in the background to bring about a web that is more open, decentralized, and just.

The founding team of the Polygon firms joined together with the shared goal of scaling Ethereum's publicly owned infrastructure and making Web3 available to everyone. We have years of experience in this field and are Ethereum enthusiasts. We think this is our best chance to build a new, decentralized network where artists and consumers may gain more control over the value they produce.

You might be able to tell that we are somewhat—okay, more than somewhat—extremely, unbelievable, jumping-out-of-our-chairs enthusiastic about Ethereum's impending switch to PoS, a method Polygon has been employing for years, on the day of the merging.

But since everyone is focused on Ethereum, we've also been asked a lot of questions about what Polygon's transition from PoW to PoS implies for Ethereum. The merger's impact on Polygon

The merge is only good news for Polygon.

The slightly more detailed response is that Ethereum will become more environmentally conscious like we are as a result of the merger. However, it won't make Ethereum faster or cut its gas fees. In order to address this, the network is dependent on Polygon and other Layer 2 solutions.

The Ethereum community, according to the Ethereum Foundation, is fully convinced that Layer 2 scaling is the sole method for resolving the scalability trilemma while maintaining security and decentralization.

The integration positions Ethereum for upcoming enhancements like sharding that will aid in its expansion and scaling. Nevertheless, Polygon should expand along with Ethereum. Every advancement made to Ethereum as a settlement layer increases Polygon's influence.

The integration arguably strengthens Ethereum's security and lowers ETH inflation while addressing Ethereum's enormous carbon footprint. Despite the fact that Ethereum greatly benefits from the Polygon companies' range of scaling solutions, including the recently unveiled Polygon zkVM, Polygon still benefits from Ethereum's increased security and overall ecosystem expansion.

Proof of stake alters this story, making Ethereum into a network that is substantially more ecologically friendly than Polygon.

Your go-to guide for a high-level explanation of the switch to PoS will be this post. You'll discover why, going forward, Polygon will be even more vital to the health of the larger Ethereum ecosystem.

At the moment, proof of work is how Ethereum protects its network, verifies data, and stores it on the blockchain. In order to publish new blocks, a decentralized, dispersed network of miners invests enormous amounts of energy in competing to be the first to solve challenging mathematical puzzles. As a result, they get paid transaction fees and prizes.

The PoW consensus mechanism in Ethereum encourages a decentralized network, similar to Bitcoin. However, PoW achieves this by essentially swapping energy (effort) for money (ETH).

By switching to PoS, Ethereum will consume 99.95% less energy while also enhancing security against concerted attacks and decentralizing the network. In a time when reducing CO2 emissions is more important than ever, Ethereum becomes future-proof, much like Polygon.

The merger is in accordance with our objective of becoming a carbon-negative chain by the end of 2022 and our Green Manifesto.

PoS depends on validators rather than how much energy miners consume.

A minimum of 32 ETH must be placed as a "stake" in a smart contract, acting something like a deposit of ETH into a safe, in order to become a validator. Validators ensure the validity of each block by proposing and voting on data that is released to the network. Instead of relying on the quantity of energy that mining rigs produce, security now depends on the total amount of ETH staked. Over 413,000 validators have so far staked nearly 14 million ETH in exchange for rewards for protecting the network. Through staking pools, anyone with any amount of ETH can contribute to security and, in exchange, receive a share of the benefits from their validator.

All of this is fantastic news that paves the way for Ethereum's surge phase, which includes advancements like sharding.

But we're not there yet. And even when Ethereum does increase network capacity in the future, it will only amplify Polygon in parallel–helping Polygon become the go-to transaction layer for users and builders

According to the strategy for Ethereum, the network will serve as a settlement layer for Layer 2 solutions like Polygon. Ethereum's core developers envisage it as the basis from which L2s will derive their security and publish transactions.

Polygon's benefits, such as its speed, cheap transaction costs, and user-friendliness, which help make Web3 a reality, are greatly amplified by any expansion in the settlement layer.

Ethereum and Polygon both have a bright future. We have created cutting-edge technology with the recent Polygon zkVM breakthrough that will process transactions at significantly higher speeds and lower costs—essential for bringing a billion users into the Ethereum ecosystem.

After our celebration, we must return to work. We have a laser-like focus on being the world's quickest, safest destination for users, builders, and dApp developers.

Chapter 4: Ethereum price prediction: What happens after The Merge

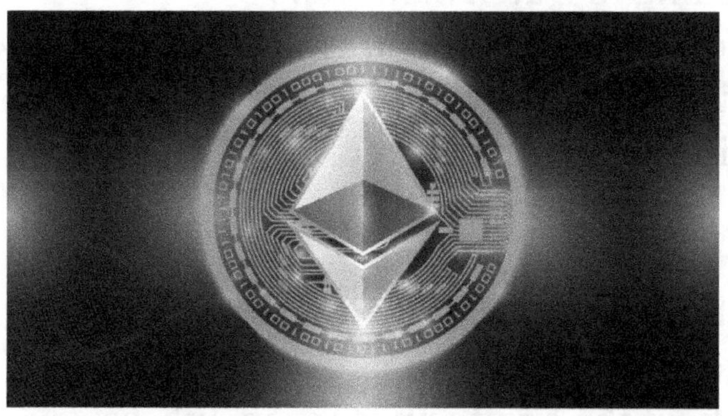

Finally, Ethereum's (ETH) switch from the proof-of-work (PoW) consensus method to the proof-of-stake (PoS) consensus mechanism has taken place. The transition, known as "The Merge," is a feature of Ethereum 2.0.

Considering how volatile cryptocurrencies are, there is a lot of conjecture about what will happen after The Merge. In actuality, no one is certain, although there are several alternatives.

According to Dutch bank Saxo's cryptocurrency expert, Mads Eberhardt, anticipation of the update has caused bitcoin values to climb recently.

“Trading favors holding Ethereum on The Merge unquestionably, as seen by the price activity of the cryptocurrency in July as opposed to that of bitcoin. "We believe that the bullish attitude in Ethereum has positively impacted the price actions of the market's other cryptocurrencies, including Bitcoin," Eberhardt stated in an update on August 1st, 2022.

The Merge, which was ultimately finished at roughly 7.45 am on September 15, 2022, was referred to in the past by Eberhardt as "one of the most consequential events in the history of crypto by influencing Ethereum both technically and commercially."

What is The Merge, and how will it affect the trajectory of the price of Ether, the native coin of Ethereum? In this post, we examine the most recent changes in the PoS transition and other elements that may affect the Ethereum price forecast as of September 15, 2022.

How will The Merge change Ethereum's operation?

The Ethereum blockchain will change how transactions are verified after PoS replaces PoW. Miners will stake the native Ethereum token, ETH, to the network instead of using a lot of computational power to validate and construct new blocks, significantly lowering the amount of energy used.

"For Ethereum, a new block is currently completed every 13 seconds or so. Every miner competes to be the one to complete the block in these 13 seconds. According to Saxo's Eberhardt, electricity is needed because this entails using computational power.

“However, in the end, it is solely one miner that finalises the block and verifies the transactions, even though other miners have spent a tremendous amount of energy on the same block.

"In terms of proof-of-stake, one validator is randomly chosen to finalise a block based on the amount of ether staked. This happens prior to the block, so no other stalker is trying to finalise the same block, ultimately reducing Ethereum's energy consumption by around 99.95%. "

PoS will also improve the economics of the Ethereum blockchain, as under PoW, Ethereum issues 5.4 million ETH to miners annually, but it will only issue around 500,000 ETH to stakers. This will reduce inflation and could see Ether become deflationary as a portion of the fees for each transaction will be burned, lowering the coin's overall supply.

Holders of ETH shouldn't be affected by The Merge in any other way. It is not anticipated to have an impact on tokens or blockchain-based smart contracts. Applications that are decentralized (dApps) ought to continue to operate normally.

The Merge shouldn't materially improve Ethereum's scalability because shards, which divide a blockchain into smaller portions, will be introduced in 2019.

When sharding is finished in 2023, ETH's speed will be increased to 100,000 transactions per second from its present limit of merely 25. Additionally, it will lower petrol prices, lowering transaction costs.

On June 8, 2022, on the Ropsten test network, the Ethereum development team successfully completed the first public test of The Merge (testnet). Developers may test new features on testnets, which are essentially exact replicas of blockchains, before integrating them into the mainnet, the operational blockchain network. Testnets increase with time, which makes them more difficult to maintain because they are full-scale blockchains.

The Ethereum Foundation, which oversees the network's development, declared on June 21st, 2022, that Ropsten and two further testnets will be discontinued following The Merge.

Shortly after the switch to PoS, the Kiln Merge testnet, which was established earlier in 2022, will be terminated. Before switching to PoS, Ropsten was Ethereum's longest-running PoW testnet. It will be shut down in the fourth quarter of 2022. In the second or third quarter of 2023, Rinkeby, a proof-of-authority testnet, will be shut down without switching to PoS.

Two further testnets, Goerli (or Görli), and Sepolia, will be maintained for the long term after the closing of the three testnets. According to the foundation, Goerli will combine with the Prater Beacon Chain testnet, and a new Beacon Chain has been made to convert Sepolia to PoS.

Sepolia was the second Ethereum test network to successfully switch to PoS without encountering any significant issues at the beginning of July. The Goerli testnet merging is slated for a block on the chain that will likely be reached between August 6 and August 12, according to a statement made by the Ethereum Foundation on July 27.

The Ethereum Foundation predicted that the update would be finished in its entirety by September 20 at some time. It finally happened on the morning of September 15.

ETH price around the merge

Despite The Merge's impending arrival, the price of ETH fell precipitously in the first half of the year as cryptocurrency markets became negative, particularly in the wake of the collapse of the TerraUSD stablecoin (UST) and its companion LUNA token in May.

Beginning the year with $3,683.05, the price of ETH increased till it reached $3,876.79 on January 4, 2022. Following a downward trend, it fell to $2,172.30 on January 24 as the cryptocurrency markets collapsed. On February 10, the currency rose to $3,271.32; however, on February 24, 2022, it had fallen to $2,308.91.

The market made another attempt to mount a comeback on April 3, 2022, but ETH was unable to hold onto the gains and once again began to decline. The Terra meltdown caused the price of ETH to go below $2,000, reaching $1,748.30 on May 12.

The price dropped to $896.11 on June 18, 2022, its lowest level since late 2020, as a result of more selling. After the Ethereum Foundation confirmed on July 27 that the Goerli merger would proceed, the market then surged, rising by 98% from that low to a high of $1,774.58 on July 28, 2022, according to ETH price data.

The price of the currency has subsequently dropped somewhat, and it hit a low of

$1,500.01 on September 7 until news of the Bellatrix upgrade's completion and the revelation that Swiss bank SEBA will provide its clients access to ETH staking caused it to trade at roughly $1,625 on September 8 morning 2022.

The next day, in the afternoon, they found it to be worth roughly $1,720. This price appeared following the announcement that the Kiln, Ropsten, and Rinkeby testnets would be shut down.

Over the weekend, Google added a counter to its Ethereum Merge search page that indicated The Merge would occur in the early hours of September 15. ETH's value was about $1,710 on September 13; however, due to market circumstances, it dropped significantly over the course of the next 24 hours, and on September 14, it was approximately $1,610.

The currency increased after the conclusion of the Merge was announced, so on September 15, 2022, it was selling at around $1,640.Over the weekend, Google added a counter to its Ethereum Merge search page that indicated The Merge would occur in the early hours of September 15. ETH's value was about $1,710 on September 13; however, due to market circumstances, it dropped significantly over the course of the next 24 hours, and on September 14, it was approximately $1,610.

The currency increased after the conclusion of the Merge was announced, so on September 15, 2022, it was selling at around $1,640.

What might happen after The Merge?

Although the markets and many ETH investors have been anticipating the merger, the blockchain's miners have expressed some worry since they stand to lose a sizable amount of potential money once the conversion to proof-of-stake is made.

Because of this, a group of miners came up with ETHW, a variant of Ethereum that would function via a proof-of-work consensus method. The organization, going by the name ETHW Core, stated on September 12 that their mainnet would launch 24 hours after The Merge.

After The Merge had occurred, the group's Twitter account verified this, having only recently issued a list of mining pools. Although this will not be the first time that ETH has undergone a split, it will be worthwhile monitoring any developments on that front. For instance, one such fork contributed to the creation of the Ethereum Classic (ETC) cryptocurrency.

Another thing we must emphasize is that there will be hazards associated with The Merge. For instance, the blockchain can cease operations or validators might band together to do malevolent acts, harming the system's standing.

Additionally, without proof-of-work, it could just end up being another proof-of-stake blockchain, similar to those of its rivals like Solana (SOL), Polkadot (DOT), or Avalanche (AVAX).

However, companies such as Tron (TRX), Tezos (XTZ), and Algorand (ALGO) may benefit as well. Even if the prices of the six cryptocurrencies we've discussed have all decreased over the past three months, there is still a chance that The Merge will be advantageous for them.

It's also possible that anything may go wrong as a result of The Merge, seriously harming Ethereum's image. If that occurs, it is likely that investors and developers will look for someone or something to hold accountable.

This may very well turn out to be Ethereum itself, which might result in investors withdrawing their funds and perhaps triggering a collapse that would obliterate the cryptocurrency market.

Additionally, if something goes wrong as a result of the merge, it might result in a significant liquidity drain, which could then cause DeFi prices to become extremely volatile.

Additionally, there is the issue of non-fungible tokens (NFTs). Due to the fact that most, if not all, NFTs are built on Ethereum, the possibility of many forks may make it difficult for some NFT holders to determine exactly what they possess and where it is. This might therefore fuel the proliferation of NFT frauds when products are falsely posted as being for sale.

However, the threat of scams is not limited to the NFT market; there is also a chance that fraudulently announced airdrops and support scams might defraud users of their money.

Ethereum's estimated priceWhat is the forecast for the price of Ethereum in the run-up to The Merge and in the future? Let's look at some of the estimates for the price of ether as of September 15, 2022.
Remember that price predictions are frequently off. It's also crucial to keep in mind that long-term crypto price forecasts are frequently created using an algorithm, which means they might be altered at any time.

As of September 14, 2022, the analysis provided by CoinCodex indicated that the short-term outlook for the ETH price remained unfavorable. The website's forecast for the price of Ethereum's

cryptocurrency was likewise negative; it predicted that it would climb to $1,370.46 by September 20 and then perhaps rebound to $1,444.49 by October 16.
According to Gov Capital's price forecast for 2022, Ethereum would cost $2,056.89 at the end of the year, $4,553.10 less by the end of 2023, and $10,870.67 less by the end of 2025.

Gov Capital's estimate of Ether's price for 2025 was higher than DigitalCoin Price, which was $6,458.60. The price was predicted to be $2,108.05 on average in 2022, $3,615.60 in 2023, and $4,994.18 in 2024. According to historical data, the website predicts that the average price in 2030 will be $22,254.64.

PricePrediction maintained an extremely positive long-term Ethereum forecast based on artificial intelligence-assisted technical research, projecting that ETH may average $1,952.15 in 2022, $2,926.10 in 2023, and

$6,421.33 in 2025. According to the website's forecast, the price of Ethereum might reach $39,995.93 in 2030.

It's critical to bear in mind that cryptocurrency markets continue to be incredibly unpredictable, making it challenging to anticipate a coin's price with any degree of accuracy over the short term and even harder to provide projections for the long term.

As a result, forecasts made by experts and algorithm-based forecasters occasionally turn out to be inaccurate. We advise you to do your own research if you're thinking about buying cryptocurrency tokens. Before making any investing or trading choices, consider the most recent market trends, news, technical and fundamental analysis, and analyst comments.

Never invest money that you cannot afford to lose, since previous success is not a guarantee of future results.

www.ingramcontent.com/pod-product-compliance
Lightning Source LLC
LaVergne TN
LVHW050341160826
845677LV00014B/3723

* 9 7 9 8 3 5 3 2 4 3 9 3 9 *